My Day

Rod Campbell

PictureLions
An Imprint of HarperCollins*Publishers*

I'm getting up.
I can name lots of things.
Follow me and see
if you can too.

I get dressed

vest

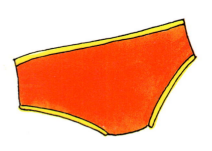

pants

shirt

dress

trousers

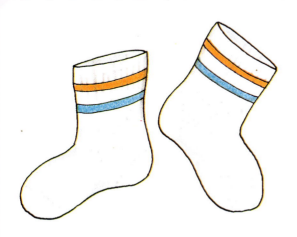

socks

shoes

My house

lamp

chair

cushion

television

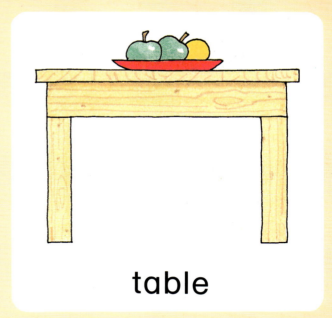

table

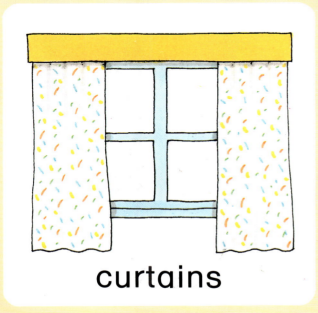

curtains

picture

fridge

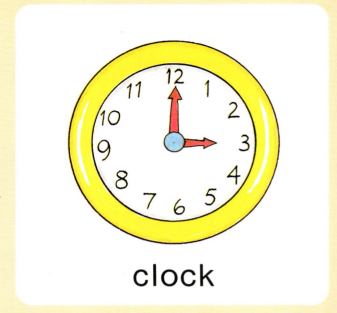

clock

kettle

dustpan
and brush

washing machine

toaster

vacuum
cleaner

iron

My garden

watering can

butterfly

bird

ladybird

wall

wheelbarrow

frog

My toys

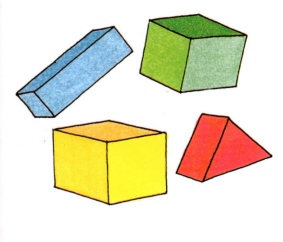

bricks

ball

rocking horse

doll

drum

telephone

car

I go shopping

money

shopping bag

woolly hat

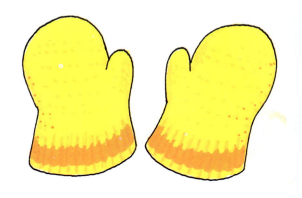

mittens

bus

car

aeroplane

keys

glasses

camera

ice-cream

balloon

cake

plant

letter

At the park

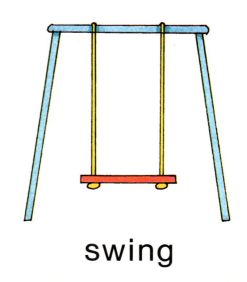

swing

dog

duck

tree

leaves

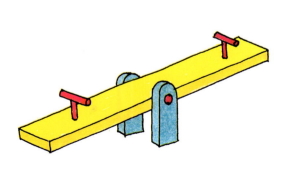

seesaw

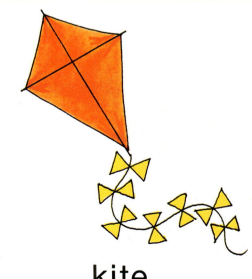

kite

In the countryside

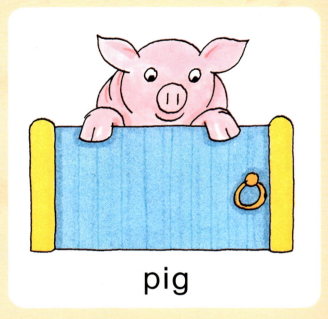

pig

cow

sheep

hen

chicks

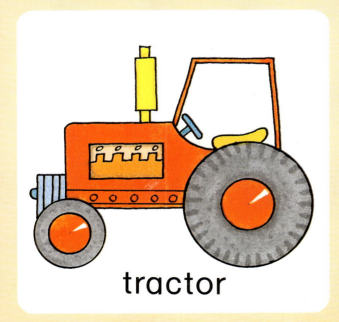

tractor

horse

At the zoo

DO NOT FEED THE ANIMALS!

lion

giraffe

elephant

monkey

camel

penguin

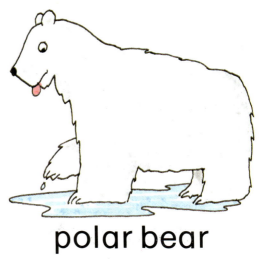

polar bear

My tea-time

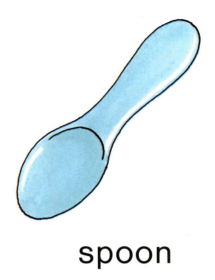

spoon

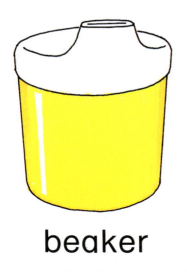

beaker

egg

plate

bread

jug

jam

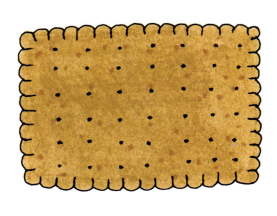

biscuit

fruit drink

jelly

cake

banana

apple

yoghurt

orange

My bedtime

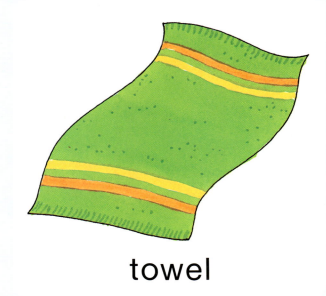

towel

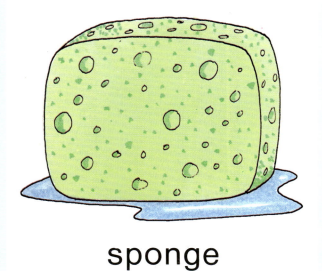

sponge

toothbrush

potty

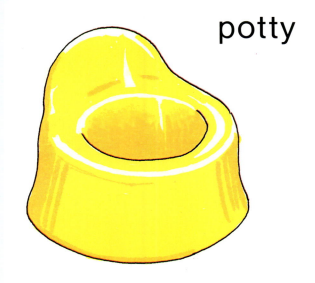

slippers

teddy

book

I'm going to sleep now.
Goodnight!

First published in Great Britain by
William Collins Sons & Co Ltd 1986
First published in Picture Lions 1986
This edition 1991
Picture Lions is an imprint of the Children's
Division, part of HarperCollins Publishers Ltd
77/85 Fulham Palace Road, Hammersmith,
London W6 8JB

Printed in Great Britain by
BPCC Hazell Books. Paulton and Aylesbury